LANDF🌎RMS

ISLANDS

THOMAS F. SHEEHAN

Rourke

Publishing LLC
Vero Beach, Florida 32964

www.rourkepublishing.com

Page 4 © V. J. Matthew, Thor Jorgen Udvang; Page 5 © iofoto; Page 6 © Armin Rose, Miguel Angelo Silva; Page 8 © Andrea Haase, Vaide Seskauskiene; Page 10 © Bryan Busovicki, Lukás Hejtman; Page 13 © Albo; Page 16 © Stanislav Komogorov, Vladimir Melnik, Jim Lipschutz, Martin Strmiska; Page 17 © Lawrence Cruciana, Ian Scott; Page 19 © NOAA; Page 20 © Hiroshi Sato, Ian Scott, Khoroshunova Olga, Kanu Suguro; Page 21 © Cornelis Opstal; Page 22 © Gail Johnson; Page 23 © Muriel Lasure, Andreas Gradin, Jens Stolt; Page 24 © ALBERTO POMARES; Page 25 © FloridaStock; Page 26 © Jose Alberto Tejo; Page 27 © Gail Johnson, Ian Scott, Sebastian Duda; Page 28 © Leo, Cheryl Casey; Page 29 © emin kuliyev, Boleslaw Kubica, Anita
Pg 30 Erik Courtney

Design, Production and Editorial - Blue Door Publishing; bdpublishing.com

Library of Congress Cataloging-in-Publication Data

Sheehan, Thomas F., 1939-
 Islands / Thomas F. Sheehan.
    p. cm. -- (Landforms)
 ISBN 978-1-60044-545-3 (Hard cover)
 ISBN 978-1-60044-706-8 (Soft cover)
1. Islands--Juvenile literature. I. Title.
 GB471.S54 2008
 551.42--dc22
                                    2007012183

ig/ig

Printed In The USA

Table Of Contents

What do You Know About Islands?

Do you live on an island? If so, you are probably used to traveling over bridges, through tunnels, or riding on ferryboats to get to other places. That's because islands are pieces of land that are completely surrounded by water. Continents are surrounded by water, too. But islands are much smaller than continents.

Bridges and boats are two ways to get to and from islands.

A small island in the Caribbean.

People are fascinated with islands. You may visit an island someday. You may go for the sandy beaches, the mountainous terrain, or the good fishing and diving.

Islands offer people a way to enjoy the water and unique landscapes.

There are two kinds of islands; continental islands and oceanic islands.

Lets take a trip around the world and visit some of these islands.

Fishing from a sandy island beach.

A cold water arctic island.

Island ecosystems are interesting and fun to learn about. Islands can be mountainous and rocky, volcanoes spewing lava, or flat and sandy. Islands can

A warm water tropical island.

have grass and plants, just like the ones where you live.

Some islands are surrounded by deep, cold water and others are surrounded by shallow, warm water.

ISLAND TRIVIA

Did you know that there are no size restrictions on what makes an island? That means that every land mass on Earth could be considered an island.

Continental Islands

There are many types of continental islands. continental islands are pieces of land that form on an underwater land mass called the continental shelf. A continental shelf is an underwater area that extends outward from a continent. After sloping off, it eventually drops off to the deep ocean basin.

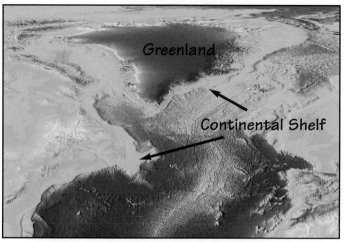

The light blue color shows the continental shelf.

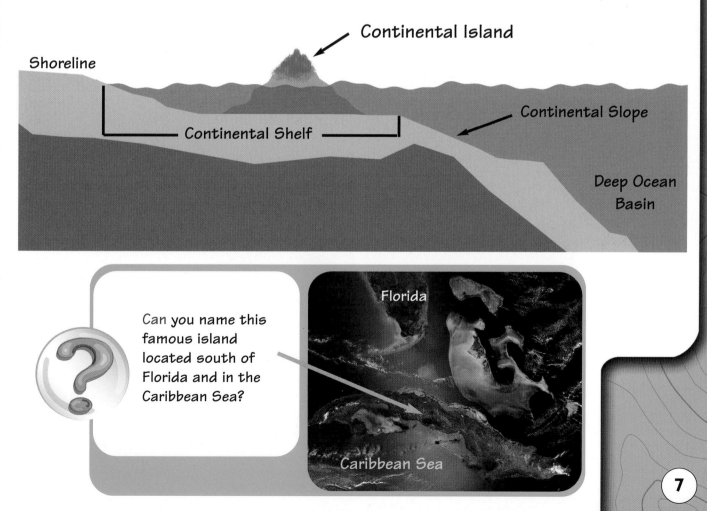

Shoreline

Continental Island

Continental Shelf

Continental Slope

Deep Ocean Basin

Can you name this famous island located south of Florida and in the Caribbean Sea?

Florida

Caribbean Sea

How Do Continental Islands Form?

Continental islands are formed in many ways. Some are the result of rifting, an effect that pushes land upward forming mountains and valleys. As they lift over time, some mountains begin to stick out of the water creating islands. Continental islands also form when water currents along a coastline pick up silt and sand from the continental shelf. The silt and sand builds up in places along the coast creating sandy islands called barrier islands.

Many continental islands were once part of a larger piece of land. Thousands of years of erosion has worn away the land and created an island.

Continental islands form as large rocky islands like England or small sandy islands.

There are many well-known pieces of land that are considered continental islands. Greenland, Barbados, Great Britain, Ireland, and Sicily to name a few.

The Great Barrier Reef is also a continental island. It, like Ireland, was once connected to a larger piece of land or continent.

Great Barrier Reef

Australia

A satellite image shows the Great Barrier Reef, a string of islands and the reefs, that were once connected to Australia.

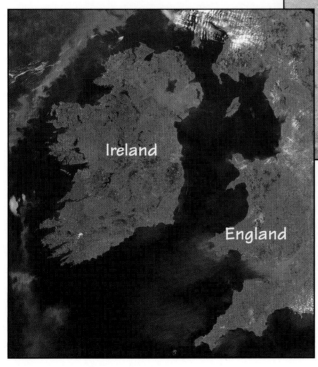

Ireland

England

Ireland and England were once connected to the large land mass called Europe.

An islet is a very small island composed of rock or sand. It is uninhabited and generally has little or no vegetation.

Oceanic Islands

Most oceanic islands are volcanic in nature. They do not sit on continental shelves. Unlike the continental islands, oceanic islands have never been connected to a continent. They form or grow from the ocean floor.

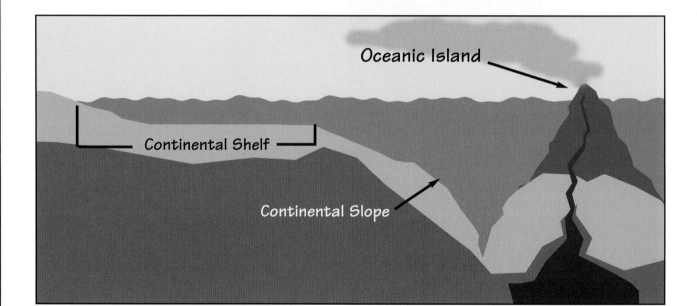

Mount Kilauea in Hawaii continues to flow lava into the ocean making the island grow larger each year.

Oceanic Island

Continental Shelf

Continental Slope

Did you know that volcanoes form under the ocean surface the exact same way they form on land?

How Do Oceanic Islands Form?

Just like continental islands, there are several ways oceanic islands form. Oceanic islands form through the collisions of two plates, rifting, or volcanic hot spots.

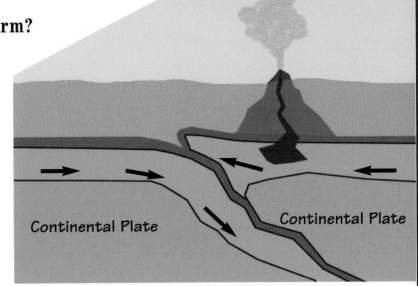

When two continental plates collide, one is usually driven below the other. When there is volcanic activity in these spots, islands can form. This is known as continental collision. The result is an oceanic island.

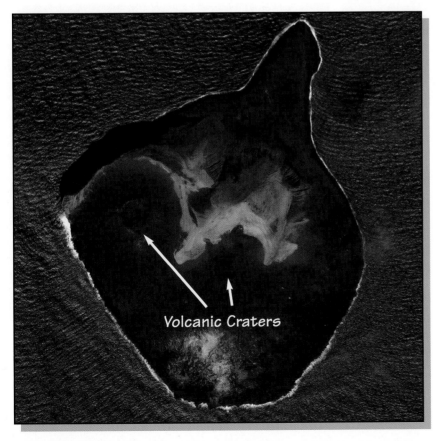

Volcanic Craters

A fisherman originally spotted this island in 1963. It was a cloud of dirt and smoke coming off the ocean's surface. Today, it is an oceanic island that is starting to grow vegetation.

Greenland is the largest volcanic island on Earth. It was created by oceanic rifting and sits right on top of the Mid Atlantic Ridge.

Another way oceanic islands form is through the process of oceanic rifting. This is where two underwater plates are moving away from eah other.

The third way a oceanic island is formed is through volcanic hot spots—island that were once a volcano. These types are usually found in strings of several islands lined up in a row.

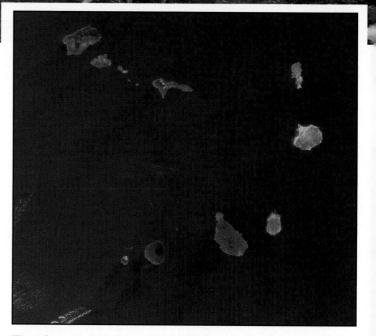

The Cape Verde Islands lie off the coast of Africa. They are steep and rocky. The islands are often hit by dust storms blowing from the Sahara Desert.

Atolls

Atolls are some of the most amazing and complex structures on Earth. These islands and island complexes support a large number of fish species and invertebrates.

An atoll is created when a coral reef builds up around an island. This can take thousands of years. As the island begins to erode away, the coral reef remains often leaving behind a ring-shaped coral and sand island. Atolls come in all shapes and sizes. Some are large enough to be seen from space.

Like many oceanic islands, atolls often form well away from any landmass. In fact, they can be surrounded by water that is thousands of feet deep.

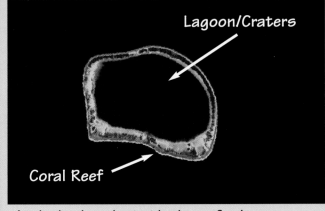

Lagoon/Craters

Coral Reef

As the land erodes inside the reef, a lagoon or crater is often left behind.

These amazing islands, seen from a satellite, show the many different shapes and sizes of atolls.

13

Island Cays

Cays or keys as they are pronounced, are islands made up of coral and sand. They form over long periods of time and can be any size and shape. Ocean currents are usually responsible for their formation. The stronger the current or tide, the larger the cay may grow.

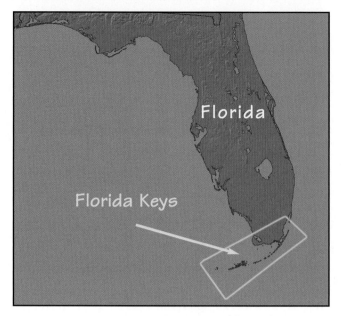

There are cays all over the world but the term is usually associated with the Caribbean region. This includes the southern most portion of Florida in an area called the Florida Keys.

This satellite image shows the string of islands coming off the south coast of Florida and the clear, warm tropical waters that surround them.

The Florida Keys consist of about 1700 islands in the Southeastern United States. They begin at the southeastern tip of the Florida peninsula. South Florida used to be underwater until about 100,000 years ago when sea levels had dropped enough to uncover it. The Keys are made up of ancient coral reefs which died and hardened when they were no longer underwater.

Archipelagos

Archipelagos are islands that form in groups or strings. They are usually formed by underwater volcanoes and often along underwater mid-ocean ridges. Although weathering and erosion also plays a role in the process. Archipelagos form all over the world. One of the most famous is the Hawaiian Islands. The largest Archipelago formation, by number of islands, is off the coast of Finland in the Archipelago Sea.

Islands of the Archipelago Sea

Many of the islands in the Archipelagos Sea are small and uninhabited. If every island was counted, the total number would be close to 50,000.

Hawaiian Islands

The Hawaiian Islands still have active volcanoes. They are located in the Pacific Ocean and 1,300 miles from the nearest continent. They are the most isolated islands on Earth.

archipelago (ar kuh PEL uh goh)

An island reef made of rock.

An island reef made of sand.

A island reef made of coral.

Island Reefs

Reefs are some of the most amazing structures on Earth. They come in all shapes and sizes and can be made of rock, sand, or living coral. Coral reefs are the most abundant and well-known.

Most reefs lie just below the surface. Coral reefs will generally not be found below 100 feet where light is dim and temperatures are cooler. It is also common for reefs to be seen above the water's surface during low tides.

Reefs can be good news or bad news. Reefs are good since they protect islands and are home to all types of sea life. They can be bad or dangerous when ships try to navigate around them. Ships often run into reefs and sink.

As the tide drops, this coral reef will become exposed.

Some of the most famous shipwrecks in our history were caused by a ship running into a reef. There are historic records dating back to the 1600's telling of ships hitting reefs and sinking. Some of these ships have been recovered, and millions of dollars of treasures found.

Many are still out there.

Shipwrecks often become artificial reefs. Sea life will feed upon and make homes out of sunken ships. After a period of time, the salt water will rot away the wood and metal leaving behind a newly formed reef community.

Modern day ships still run aground, sink and become an artificial reef.

Brain coral, and other reef sea life, have made their home on a sunken ship's steel beam.

Tropical Coral Reefs

Tropical coral reefs are some of the most colorful living things on Earth. They are mostly found in the warm shallow waters of the tropics. Coral reefs are structures made from living organisms called corals. To create the reef, corals produce a type of calcium that makes a hard skeleton. The calcium material builds up over time and becomes home to thousands of marine mammals.

From the air you can clearly see the coral reef that surrounds this island.

The best way to see a coral reef is from below the surface. This means putting on diving gear or maybe just a mask and snorkel. Many reefs are shallow and easy to see by swimming along the surface.

Whatever way you decide, local dive shops can help. They will take you out with a group and teach you about the island's local reefs and its inhabitants.

This coral reef is easy to get to and perfect for swimming around or snorkeling.

Many kinds of colorful fish invertebrates and corals can be found on island reefs all over the world.

Polar Region

Temperate Region

Tropical Region

Temperate Region

Polar Region

Temperate Reefs

Since islands form all over the world, it is natural that reefs would form with them. The reefs that form around temperate climate islands are home to different species than those in tropical waters. Temperate region islands are in an area on Earth between the tropical and polar zones. The large island of Greenland sits partially in the temperate region and partially in the polar region.

There are many well-known temperate climate reefs including those off the coast of the United Kingdom.

Can you name a famous coral reef that lies off the coast of Australia?

A Cuttlefish swims along an island reef in the cold North Atlantic water.

Island Plants and Animals

The kinds of plants and animals you will find on and around an island depends largely on the type of island. Cold, polar islands will have plants and animals that have adapted to icy temperatures. Warm, tropical islands will have plants and animals that can survive hot or humid climates. Oceanic islands near continents may have continental plants and animals. Some islands may have endemic species.

Komodo Dragons only naturally inhabit the islands of Komodo, Rinca, Padar, Flores, Gili Motang, Owadi, and Samiin in central Indonesia.

endemic (en DEM ik)
naturally found in one particular place and nowhere else.

The Haleakala silversword is endemic to the island of Maui.

Baobab tree

The fossa is the largest mammalian carnivore on Madagascar.

~Madagascar~

Madagascar is the fourth largest island in the world. It is located in the Indian Ocean, off the southeastern coast of Africa. It is home to many endemic species. Among these are lemurs, fossas (pronounced foussas), and six types of baobab trees.

A *ring-tailed lemur*

Africa

Madagascar

Most tropical islands have the perfect conditions for growing plants and trees—lots of moisture and plenty of sun. Palm trees are common on tropical islands. There are thousands of different kinds of palm trees. Bananas, plantains, pineapples, and mangoes are just some of the fruit that like tropical climates.

Mangroves are a kind of tree that can live in salt water. They often grow along the coasts of many tropical islands. This picture shows the mangroves' special kinds of roots that stick up out of the water to get oxygen. Mangroves help protect island shorelines from erosion. Their roots help hold sand and mud in place and keep the ocean from washing it away. Mangroves are also habitats for many kinds of fish, shellfish, and crabs.

Mangroves growing around a tropical island.

We often think of islands as being located in warm tropical waters. In fact, islands form all over the world, including polar regions. Many plants and animals have adapted to living on these cold polar islands.

You can also find arctic archipelagos like the Canadian Arctic Archipelago. This group of 36,000 islands is mostly uninhabited by people. In the summer months, many arctic islands come alive with a variety of plant and animal life.

Greenland in winter.

Arctic tundra moss and berries.

An arctic fox gets a break from winter.

~The Galápagos Islands~

The Galápagos Islands are about 600 miles (965 k) west of Ecuador, South America, in the Pacific Ocean. They are an archipelago of volcanic islands. There are 3 main islands, 6 smaller islands, and 107 rocks and islets.

The Galápagos Islands are famous for having many animals that are not found naturally anywhere else. One of the most well-known animal species on the islands is the Galápagos giant tortoise. These tortoises can grow to 3.9 feet (1.2 m) long and weigh over 660 lb (300 k).

A blue-footed booby. One of the many bird species that like to nest on the Galápagos Islands.

Not all plants and animals survive by living on an island. Some survive by living in the waters around an island.

Walruses, polar bears, penguins, crabs, and many other animals spend a great deal of time on an island as well as in the surrounding waters. Sharks, dolphins, manatees, fish, and hundreds of other species spend much of their time in the waters surrounding an island.

A blacktip shark cruises around an island reef in search of a meal.

Walruses must come ashore to rest when not hunting the ocean for food.

Islands in Danger

There are two major causes for the destruction of islands all over the world. One is natural and one is man-made.

The biggest natural cause in the destruction of islands is weathering and natural erosion. This takes place over hundreds and thousands of years. Wind and water are powerful forces and can easily reshape land. Hurricanes and tsunamis can cause instant destruction wiping out plants, animals, and people in a matter of days or hours.

Large ocean waves from an offshore hurricane pound an island shoreline.

Some beach communities put fences along their beaches. The fences act as barriers and help prevent erosion.

Manhattan Island in New York.

A bulldozer makes a new island road.

Islands are also in danger by people. People love the idea of living on an island. Some islands offer people the chance to get away from crowded cities, and to live where there is plenty of sunshine. Others love island life because it allows them quick access to water for fishing, surfing, sailing, and swimming. But not all islands are free of crowds. Manhattan, New York, for example, is one of the most populated islands on Earth.

Today, people are moving to islands in record numbers. With people comes the construction of buildings and roads, pollution, destruction of native plants, and the disappearance of island wildlife. We can all do our part to help protect our natural resources on islands, and in our own neighborhoods.

Trash laying on a beach.

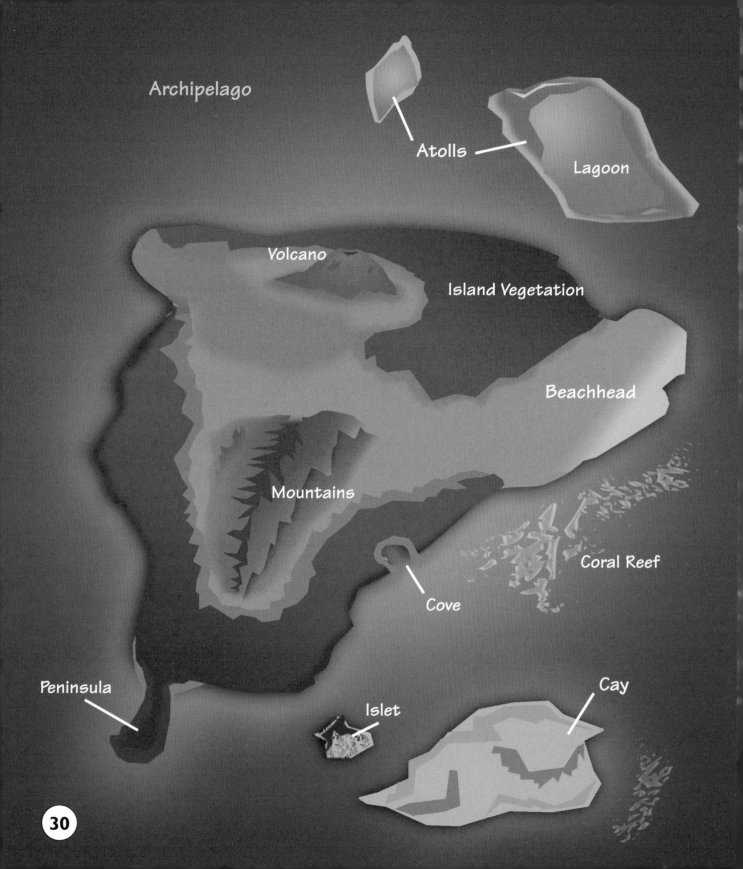

Archipelago

Atolls

Lagoon

Volcano

Island Vegetation

Beachhead

Mountains

Coral Reef

Cove

Peninsula

Islet

Cay